In a clear, challenging, yet concise way, Christine takes the truth of Scripture and her love of her dog Lad and presents practical truths for living. If you're a dog lover with an appreciation for the truth of Scripture, then you'll love this read. It's loaded with lessons that apply to everyday living. Once in Scripture, God spoke through a donkey. This time He's chosen to speak through Lad, Christine's special friend. Through this book He'll speak to you.

—**Dave Engbrecht**, *senior pastor of Nappanee Missionary Church*

One of the keys to spiritual growth is the ability to notice biblical truths in the world around us. Christine Ferris extracts from the everyday behaviors of her dog significant insights that will enrich the lives of all who read *Lessons from Lad*.

—**Terry L. Brensinger**, *author and former president, Fresno Pacific Biblical Seminary*

Being a big animal lover, I found the short stories in *Lessons from Lad* insightful and touching, bringing to our attention eternal reminders. I highly recommend this book. It will nourish your soul.

—**Anna Simpson**, *storytelling coach, helping coaches discover, clarify, and articulate their genius*

Using parables to describe each Lad Lesson, Christine Ferris has embraced "Hard Things" (Lad Lesson 23) and turned the loss of her beloved canine companion into a spiritual journey that is an inspiration to us all.

—**Nicholas Meier**, *Midwest Regional Manager, HOPE Animal Assisted Crisis Response*

In *Lessons from Lad*, Christine Ferris has woven together truth from Scripture with her experiences with her beloved Lad into a very straightforward devotional book. She writes with a warm and joyful spirit.

—**Ken Pierpont**, *lead pastor of Bethel Church*

LESSONS
FROM
Lad

CHRISTINE NICOLE FERRIS

LESSONS FROM *Lad*

WHAT MY DOG TAUGHT ME ABOUT LIFE, LOVE, LEADERSHIP, AND LOSS

© 2023 by Christine Nicole Ferris. All rights reserved.

Published by Redemption Press, PO Box 427, Enumclaw, WA 98022.

Printed in South Korea.

Redemption Press is honored to present this title in partnership with the author. The views expressed or implied in this work are those of the author. Redemption Press provides our imprint seal representing design excellence, creative content, and high-quality production.

The author has tried to recreate events, locales, and conversations from memories of them. In order to maintain their anonymity, in some instances the names of individuals, some identifying characteristics, and some details such as physical properties, occupations, and places of residence may have been changed.

Noncommercial interests may reproduce portions of this book without the express written permission of the author, provided the text does not exceed five hundred words. When reproducing text from this book, include the following credit line: "*Lessons from Lad* by Christine Nicole Ferris. Used by permission."

Commercial interests: No part of this publication may be reproduced in any form, stored in a retrieval system, or transmitted in any form by any means—electronic, photocopy, recording, or otherwise—without prior written permission of the publisher/author, except as provided by United States of America copyright law.

Unless otherwise indicated, all Scripture quotations are from the New King James Version®. Copyright © 1982 by Thomas Nelson. Used by permission. All rights reserved.

Scripture quotations marked (NIV) are from the Holy Bible, New International Version®, NIV®. Copyright © 1973, 1978, 1984, 2011 by Biblica, Inc.™ Used by permission of Zondervan. All rights reserved worldwide. www.zondervan.com. The "NIV" and "New International Version" are trademarks registered in the United States Patent and Trademark Office by Biblica, Inc.™

Scripture quotations marked (NASB) are from the (NASB®) New American Standard Bible®, Copyright © 1960, 1971, 1977, 1995, 2020 by The Lockman Foundation. Used by permission. All rights reserved. www.lockman.org.

Scripture quotations marked (AMPC) are from the Amplified® Bible, Copyright © 1954, 1958, 1962, 1964, 1965, 1987 by The Lockman Foundation. Used by permission. www.lockman.org.

Scripture quotations marked (KJV) are from the King James Version, public domain.

ISBN 13: 978-1-64645-810-3 (Hardback)
978-1-64645-812-7 (ePub)

Library of Congress Catalog Card Number: 2023900935

Lovingly dedicated to my beloved nephew, Matthew David, who was and always will be "Lad's Boy," and to all who have suffered the loss of something precious.

CONTENTS

Foreword 11
Preface 12
Acknowledgments 13
Lad Lesson 1: Keep Your Paws Clean 16
Lad Lesson 2: Pose for Pictures 18
Lad Lesson 3: Conquer Yourself First 20
Lad Lesson 4: Tell Yourself No 22
Lad Lesson 5: Be Playful 24
Lad Lesson 6: Be Nosy 26
Lad Lesson 7: Answer Softly 28
Lad Lesson 8: Be "Touchy" 30
Lad Lesson 9: Love Learning 32
Lad Lesson 10: Be Curious 34
Lad Lesson 11: Lean into Discipline 36
Lad Lesson 12: Feel Deeply 38
Lad Lesson 13: Never Give Up 40
Lad Lesson 14: Tend Your Flock 42
Lad Lesson 15: Face Your Fears 44
Lad Lesson 16: Treasure Today 46
Lad Lesson 17: Learn to Rest 48
Lad Lesson 18: Answer the Call 50
Lad Lesson 19: Walk with Poise 52
Lad Lesson 20: Guard the Young 54
Lad Lesson 21: Think Again 56
Lad Lesson 22: Choose to Wait 58
Lad Lesson 23: Embrace Hard Things 60
Lad Lesson 24: Shape Greatness 62
Lad Lesson 25: Be Gentled 64

Lad Lesson 26: Walk Softly 66
Lad Lesson 27: Love Fiercely 68
Lad Lesson 28: Be All In 70
Lad Lesson 29: Be Inclusive 72
Lad Lesson 30: Trust through Pain 74
Lad Lesson 31: Be Tall Inside 76
Lad Lesson 32: Be Helpful 78
Lad Lesson 33: Press Pause 80
Lad Lesson 34: Notice the Little Things 82
Lad Lesson 35: Ask Why 84
Lad Lesson 36: Calmer Is Better 86
Lad Lesson 37: Life Is the Gift 88
Lad Lesson 38: Trust Your Gut 90
Lad Lesson 39: Seek Peace 92
Lad Lesson 40: Focus on the Gift 94
Lad Lesson 41: Try New Things 96
Lad Lesson 42: Forgive Quickly 98
Lad Lesson 43: Be Fully Present 100
Lad Lesson 44: Love Light 102
Lad Lesson 45: Be Merry 104
Lad Lesson 46: Share Your Toys 106
Lad Lesson 47: Be Creative 108
Lad Lesson 48: Grief Is Grief 110
Lad Lesson 49: Find Your Off Switch 112
Lad Lesson 50: Be Optimistic 114
Lad Lesson 51: Easy Isn't Always Best 116
Lad Lesson 52: Assume You Don't Know 118
Epilogue: Choose to Love Again 120
About the Author 123

FOREWORD

I have had the privilege of knowing Christine and her family for many years. They have always been a special blessing, and I have personally seen them endeavor to point others to Christ in all they do. Christine's work here is no different than her everyday journey.

Her book, *Lessons from Lad*, offers a unique window, gleaned through Lad's daily journey, into the everyday triumphs, trials, teachings, and tragedies of life. Each lesson is practical and helpful as we navigate the terrain of life, and we, too, endeavor to point others to Christ. It is rooted firmly in the Word of God, and I think it will be a blessing to anyone who will read it and allow the lessons and coordinating Scriptures to take root!

"Finally, brethren, whatsoever things are true, whatsoever things are honest, whatsoever things are just, whatsoever things are pure, whatsoever things are lovely, whatsoever things are of good report; if there be any virtue, and if there be any praise, think on these things." (Philippians 4:8 KJV)

Dr. David B. Smith
Al Smith Ministries

PREFACE

My love affair with Lad began long before he was born. The seed was first planted in my heart around the age of twelve, when I stumbled upon Albert Payson Terhune's famous book, *Lad: A Dog,* at a local flea market. The moment I cracked the cover of that book, a dream began to sprout in my heart—the dream of one day owning a rough collie and naming him Lad.

Nothing can describe the joy I felt in my heart when, more than twenty-five years later, I held my Lad in my arms for the first time on May 14, 2020. Lad represented one of my dearest childhood dreams come true, and I instantly treasured him more than any other animal I had ever owned.

In direct proportion to this joy was the immense sorrow left behind when Lad was unexpectedly snatched away from me fourteen months later. In the midst of overwhelming grief, I fell to my knees and asked the only question that came to mind: "Why? God, why would You give Lad to me if You knew he was going to be taken away?" As tears fell, two words came softly to my heart: *Lad Lessons*.

So I present to you, dear reader, the lasting legacy Lad left behind in my heart. There are fifty-two lessons in all, one to ponder every week of the year. Although each lesson can be easily read in less than three minutes, many of them may take much longer to successfully integrate into your life. For me, some of them will be a lifelong application process.

As these lessons were given to me, I now entrust them to you and invite you to let Lad leave a few lasting paw prints on your heart.

ACKNOWLEDGMENTS

A heartfelt thank-you to

- ♥ my husband, David, who has been my greatest source of comfort, encouragement, and support during every part of this publishing journey. Thank you, darling, for being my chief editor, photo editor, and catalyst for creativity. You have been the wind beneath my wings.
- ♥ my mother, Sharon Joy Schaubert, who has faithfully served as an assistant editor and has cheered me on every step of the way.
- ♥ my family, who stood beside me through the loss of Lad and supported me with their love and encouragement through the creation of *Lessons from Lad*.
- ♥ Micah Juntunen, for believing in this book and God's provision for it.
- ♥ Sara Cormany, for your faithful encouragement and step-by-step guidance.
- ♥ Tammy Baker-Schrader of Daydream Designs for completing the final design of the front cover and believing wholeheartedly in this book.

If there is anything good or praiseworthy in this work, all glory and honor belong to my Savior, the Lord Jesus Christ, who brings life out of death, light out of darkness, and beauty out of brokenness.

Dogs are gifts from God to remind us of what we have forgotten in ourselves.
—Christian Simpson

LAD LESSON 1: KEEP YOUR PAWS CLEAN

Cleanse me with hyssop, and I will be clean; wash me, and I will be whiter than snow.
—Psalm 51:7 NIV

Keep your paws clean. This was the first lesson that my little Lad taught me. As we ventured outside on the very first morning of the very first day he was with me, the moment he felt the wet dew touch his small, white paws, he dropped to the ground and licked them vigorously. He repeated this ritual every few steps until he made it back to the house.

Lad's preoccupation with keeping his paws pristine did not stop there. Throughout his life, even when it looked like an exercise in futility, Lad was fastidious about keeping his paws clean and white. Rarely did I ever need to wipe his paws. If they were dirty, he was the first to notice. His absurd obsession with keeping his paws as snow-white as possible often made me laugh.

I'm grateful to Lad for teaching me to place top priority on keeping my paws clean. Sometimes it feels pointless to live a clean life. Often, no one seems to notice the effort invested in right choices and clean living. Lad taught me that keeping "clean paws" has value whether I am in the privacy of my own home or in the public eye. It matters not because others notice, but because I have the confidence of knowing my heart is clean before God.

Lord Jesus, help me to place value on keeping a clear conscience and a clean heart. Give me a desire to do what is pleasing in Your sight. Amen.

Lad at The Resort—three months old

LAD LESSON 2: POSE FOR PICTURES

The memory of the righteous is blessed.

—Proverbs 10:7

Before we even completed the drive from his first home in North Carolina to his forever home in Indiana, Lad had already mastered the art of posing for pictures.

We kept this skill sharp by taking Sunday portraits weekly until he turned one year old. Lad sat stoically, staring at the camera with his ears standing tall during the entire photo shoot. While I struggled to maintain a perfect smile and keep my two golden retrievers propped up on either side of me, Lad posed perfectly and "smiled" for the camera.

I never imagined then that his life would span only a mere sixteen months. But how thankful I am for all those pictures we took! Even in his last moments of life, Lad mustered the strength to pose one last time for one last portrait.

I'm grateful to Lad for teaching me to always be willing to pose for a picture. Pictures are the treasures we leave behind for those who love us.

Lord Jesus, thank You for giving us portraits of Your character through Your Word. Please show me how to create memories now that will be a blessing later to those I love. Amen.

Lad's first portrait—eight weeks old

Lad's final portrait—sixteen months old

LAD LESSON 3: CONQUER YOURSELF FIRST

The meek shall inherit the earth, and shall delight themselves in the abundance of peace.
—Psalm 37:11

A crazy puppy—that's what I wanted, and that's definitely what I got when I picked Lad! Born a singleton with an iron will and fiery personality, he immediately proved to be a challenge. However, my most difficult challenge was not conquering Lad's will, but rather my own.

My first attempt at grooming Lad was greeted with snarling teeth. When I hotly reprimanded him for his ridiculous response, his temper flared even more. Losing my temper only added more fuel to Lad's fire. Clearly, my loss of emotional control was counterproductive.

Conquering Lad was relatively easy after I shifted my focus to conquering myself. He taught me that patience requires more strength than force and meekness is more powerful than anger. The calmer I remained, the more cooperative Lad became. He respected leadership that was rooted in self-control.

The more I mastered myself, the easier it was to command Lad. I'm grateful to Lad for teaching me that I must lead myself well before I can successfully lead others.

Lord Jesus, please clothe my heart with humility and help me place my strength under Your control. Amen.

Lad at work—six months old

LAD LESSON 4: TELL YOURSELF NO

But the fruit of the Spirit is love, joy, peace, longsuffering, kindness, goodness, faithfulness, gentleness, self-control. Against such there is no law.

—Galatians 5:22–23

One of the first lessons Lad learned was how to say *no* to himself. It didn't take him long to discover that the sooner he said *no* to himself, the more quickly I told him *yes*. In just a matter of weeks, Lad was so good at saying *no* to himself that I found myself mostly saying *yes* to him. The more self-control Lad exercised, the more freedom he enjoyed.

Lad's favorite pastime was running free over the rolling hills at our family property, nicknamed The Resort. The prerequisite to this privilege involved Lad practicing a few obedience skills. The faster he completed each command, the more quickly I turned him loose to play. Before long, Lad restrained himself so well that the physical limitation of the leash was no longer needed.

Lad helped me understand the power of telling myself *no* in the right areas of life. I'm grateful to Lad for teaching me that the more I say *no* to myself, the more others will say *yes* to me.

Lord Jesus, please give me the strength to say *yes* to what is pleasing to You and *no* to the things that will cause harm to myself and others. Amen.

Lad resisting the temptation of the rubber duckies—three months old

LAD LESSON 5: BE PLAYFUL

I have come that they may have life, and that they may have it more abundantly.
—John 10:10

Playful. That's what Lad was. Every day. Lad even turned work into play as he pranced next to my side in heel position or bounded my way on a recall.

Lad made sure that play never dropped too low on my priority list. He waltzed up to me with one toy, sometimes two, stuffed in his mouth. With eyes dancing, Lad pressed the toy into my lap and waited expectantly for my next move. A few moments of play went a long way in making my day brighter and better.

Lad showed me that work and play, when kept in proper balance, are complementary to each other. One enhances the other. I'm grateful to Lad for teaching me that being playful is part of living a productive life. Having fun and being fruitful are not at odds with one another. They go well together. Maybe the question "Will you play with me?" is one we should never outgrow.

Lord Jesus, thank You for giving me an abundant life. Help me to be playful in ways that brighten someone else's day. Amen.

Lad at play—eight weeks old

LAD LESSON 6: BE NOSY

A merry heart makes a cheerful countenance.

—Proverbs 15:13

Lad was nosy, but not in a demanding way. With his slender snout, Lad often weaseled his way under my arm or wedged his way into the very center of what I was doing. Then he glanced up at me curiously as if to say, "Whatcha doin'?"

Lad's uninhibited approach to life certainly kept our home lively. He never hesitated to butt into whatever was happening, confident that he was welcome and wanted. His playful personality made his participation a pleasant interruption. Lad was disruptive, but in a delightful sort of way.

I miss Lad slipping his slender nose under my elbow in the middle of dinner or desk work. Lad brought happy energy into every room he entered, and his contagious cheerfulness infected everyone around him.

I'm grateful to Lad for teaching me that being nosy is a good thing when it is done with a positive attitude that brings joy to others.

Lord Jesus, please help me to be nosy in ways that show others how valuable they are to me. Show me how to be a joyful interruption in someone's day. Amen.

Lad being "nosy" with Trouper the day we picked him up from Carter Collies

LAD LESSON 7: ANSWER SOFTLY

A soft answer turns away wrath, but a harsh word stirs up anger.

—Proverbs 15:1

Answer softly. That's what Lad taught me to do. The more heated my responses were, the less cooperative he was. His precocious personality had zero tolerance for a temper that was not under control.

Initially, Lad and I had very different definitions of fun. Lad loved latching onto my clothes as I walked. And the more temper I showed, the more tenaciously he held on. Getting his needlelike milk teeth out of the fabric of my pant leg was no easy task. But a quiet command coupled with a calm response produced much better results than yielding to anger.

Answering softly almost always feels counterintuitive at the time. Yet I can't think of one instance when a soft answer failed to help Lad simmer down and respond more positively to my leadership. Getting mad feels really good in the moment, but it always leaves a trail of regret.

I'm grateful to Lad for teaching me that being calm and assertive gains more ground than getting angry. Keeping my temper and my tongue under control in the heat of conflict is challenging, but it pays off afterward.

Lord Jesus, please give me strength to answer softly and speak words that reflect Your grace. Help me respond to others in a way that protects and preserves my relationship with them. Amen.

Lad with his Trustee mentor

LAD LESSON 8: BE "TOUCHY"

Then Jesus, moved with compassion, stretched out His hand and touched him, and said to him, "I am willing; be cleansed."

—Mark 1:41

Lad was definitely a "touchy" fellow. He was almost always touching us with at least one part of his body—his paw on our foot, his chin resting on our lap, or his body leaning up against our leg. He found creative ways every day to reach out and touch us with his love.

The kitchen is not my happy place, but Lad made it a place where I loved to be by leaning his warm body against the back of my legs while I cooked or cleaned up the kitchen. Lad had a way of making every day brighter and every task feel a little lighter with the touch of his presence.

I'm grateful to Lad for teaching me that the right kind of touch has the power to change someone's day for the better. Touch can often do what words cannot.

Lord Jesus, thank You for all the ways You have touched my life with Your love. Please show me how to touch people today in a way that demonstrates Your love and makes a joyful difference in their lives. Amen.

Lad enjoying closeness with Trustee—nine weeks old

LAD LESSON 9: LOVE LEARNING

The one who gets wisdom loves life; the one who cherishes understanding will soon prosper.
—Proverbs 19:8 NIV

Lad *loved* to learn. I can't think of a time when Lad had learning fatigue. He approached every day as a new adventure. So great was his desire to learn that I often noticed him learning even when I wasn't intentionally teaching him. Directional work, retrieving, perch training, lead training, agility—you name it, and Lad loved doing it, especially when it involved learning something new.

Lad watched keenly every time I trained Trustee and often mastered new skills just by using his powers of observation. He had an insatiable appetite for learning new things, and that made being his teacher an absolute delight.

I'm grateful to Lad for teaching me that learning makes living a daily adventure. To love learning is to engage more fully in every part of life.

Lord Jesus, please give me a heart that loves to learn and looks to You daily for the lessons You want to teach me. Amen.

Lad helping me create our first teaching video together

LAD LESSON 10: BE CURIOUS

Do nothing out of selfish ambition or vain conceit. Rather, in humility value others above yourselves, not looking to your own interests but each of you to the interests of the others.
—Philippians 2:3–4 NIV

Curiosity was one of Lad's most winsome traits. From the very beginning, he avidly observed human activity and showed a keen interest in everything that I did. Though most of my actions made little sense to him, Lad showed more interest in my life than he did his own. Consequently, I have many fond memories of him.

As a young puppy, Lad watched intently as I washed the kitchen counters, his head swinging back and forth with each sweep of my hand. He often stared at me quizzically as I worked on my computer or iPhone, as if trying to understand what was so fascinating about a lit-up screen.

Lad had a talent for making each person in our family feel special by showing interest in the things that were important to them. I'm grateful to Lad for teaching me that curiosity can be one of the most meaningful expressions of love. Being interested in others is more important than trying to be interesting to others.

Lord Jesus, please help me to be more focused on others than I am on myself and to show genuine interest in the lives of those around me. Amen.

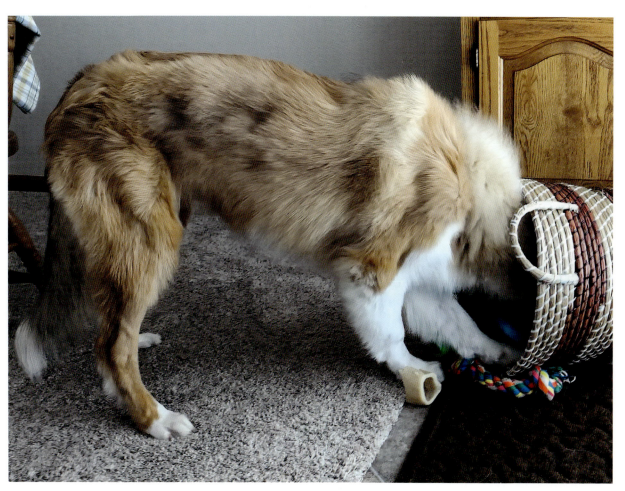

Lad's first time exploring the toy basket

LAD LESSON 11: LEAN INTO DISCIPLINE

Whoever loves discipline loves knowledge, but whoever hates correction is stupid.
—Proverbs 12:1 NIV

Lad's fiery temper was one of the first traits that stood out to us after he joined our pack. Even a simple *no* provoked him to snap repeatedly at the air in protest to the verbal restriction. We often laughed at his sassy and sometimes snarky responses. It was highly entertaining.

As Lad grew, his temper slowly gave way to a softer response to correction. Occasionally, he still resented correction, but he consistently embraced the relationship behind the reproof and demonstrated it by walking up and leaning into me.

Tears still spring to my eyes when I prep food, wash dishes, or do any number of things where Lad would usually lean into me. But my favorite memories are of the moments when he would walk up and lean into me following a moment of discipline.

I'm grateful to Lad for teaching me to lean into discipline and to place value on those who care enough to correct me when I am in the wrong.

Lord Jesus, thank You for Lad's example. Help my heart to lean into my relationship with You and to see Your discipline as a demonstration of Your love for me. Amen.

Lad's fall portrait at The Resort—six months old

LAD LESSON 12: FEEL DEEPLY

For we do not have a High Priest who cannot sympathize with our weaknesses, but was in all points tempted as we are, yet without sin.

—Hebrews 4:15

From day one, Lad was a drama king. If he liked something, he really liked it. And if he did not like something, he left no room for doubt. He let it all hang out.

Lad's dramatic responses to life provided comic relief in the otherwise monotonous doldrums of the daily grind. I grew to love his honest displays of emotion, even though they were sometimes inconvenient. Everything he felt, he felt deeply, and he made no effort to conceal it.

Lad was not only in tune with his own feelings, but he was also highly aware of the feelings of others. I'll never forget the day he abruptly got up from where he was resting and moved swiftly to my husband's side. There Lad stood, his chin resting on David's lap until the most stressful part of his virtual meeting had passed.

I'm grateful to Lad for teaching me to be transparent with and sensitive to those around me. Letting my true feelings show is a good thing as long as it is coupled with kindness toward others.

Lord Jesus, thank You for being touched by the things that touch my heart. Please give me strength to feel deeply, yet respond wisely to, whatever this day holds. Amen.

Lad at Lover's Leap in Virginia on the day we brought him home from Carter Collies

LAD LESSON 13: NEVER GIVE UP

Let us not become weary in doing good, for at the proper time we will reap a harvest if we do not give up.
—Galatians 6:9 NIV

Lad was not a quitter. He lived by the motto "If at first you don't succeed, try, try again." He was persistent, and his persistence usually paid off.

It was not uncommon for Lad to playfully thrust a toy in Trustee's face over and over again until Trustee joined his game. He had a way of nosing his way into every moment and getting the attention he desired. Even when he didn't understand what I was trying to teach him, instead of getting discouraged, he got determined.

Lad outpaced all my previous puppies in his level of training. At three months old, he could already retrieve a toy and dutifully deliver it to my hand. Lad achieved more in less time than any other puppy I have owned simply because he refused to give up.

I'm grateful to Lad for teaching me the power of perseverance. Nothing great is ever accomplished by giving up. Success has more to do with tenacity than talent.

Lord Jesus, please give me strength to press on when I feel like giving up. Help me to trust Your purposes for me and tenaciously pursue Your plan. Amen.

Lad playing a fierce game of tug with Trustee

LAD LESSON 14: TEND YOUR FLOCK

He tends his flock like a shepherd: He gathers the lambs in his arms and carries them close to his heart; he gently leads those that have young.

—Isaiah 40:11 NIV

Lad had a habit of disappearing. One minute he was right next to me, and the next moment he was gone. Countless times, I called out to other family members, "Is Lad with you?" and they always answered *yes*.

Lad kept meticulous track of his flock. If one of us wandered off, he searched for the straggler. If we were spread out, Lad bounced between locations, keeping close tabs on everyone. Lad's heart was most happy and content when we were all corralled in the same place, spending time together. He kept a sharp eye on what mattered to him most: his family.

I'm thankful to Lad for teaching me to keep a close watch on what is most precious to me. He was never too tired, too distracted, or too busy to keep us in his care.

Lord Jesus, thank You for watching over me every day and providing for my needs. Please help me to keep right priorities and watch carefully over those You have entrusted to me. Amen.

Lad with his pack at The Resort—seven months old

LAD LESSON 15: FACE YOUR FEARS

For God has not given us a spirit of fear, but of power and of love and of a sound mind.
— 2 Timothy 1:7

Lad's fear of climbing stairs grew greater with age. For some reason, nothing frightened him more than a tall flight of stairs. He was fine on the way down but came emotionally unraveled just at the thought of climbing back up. He circled the stairs, yipping in distress, before finally mustering the courage to frantically scramble to the top.

One day I decided to spend some quality time working with him one step at a time. Lad was noticeably anxious as we headed toward the bottom of the staircase but chose to trust me as I carefully placed each paw and slowly helped him make the ascent. The change didn't happen overnight, but with patient and persistent work, Lad gradually rose above his fear. Before long, he was skillfully scaling the stairs with more confidence.

I couldn't force Lad to face his fear. It was a choice only he could make. I'm thankful to Lad for teaching me that any fear can be conquered one small step at a time. When I choose to face my fears, they no longer control me, and I am able to step forward into the future with greater confidence.

Lord Jesus, You have not given me a spirit of fear. Please be with me when I am afraid, and give me courage to face and conquer the things that cause my heart to feel fearful. Amen.

Lad learning to walk a wooden plank—two months old

LAD LESSON 16: TREASURE TODAY

So teach us to number our days, that we may gain a heart of wisdom.
—Psalm 90:12

Our last Saturday evening with Lad was chock-full of recreational fun, capped by a fabulous game of keep-away. When we all nestled into bed that night, our entire pack was nicely tuckered out. Our hearts were full, and all was peaceful and well.

The next day, our world turned upside down when Lad suddenly fell to the floor in a grand mal seizure. It was one of at least two violent seizures that ravaged his body as the evening progressed.

Lad's ear-piercing cries punctuated our drive to the emergency veterinary clinic. After several hours of evaluation and testing, no definite cause could be found. With heavy hearts, we made the weary trek home in the middle of the night as Lad continued his cries of distress. We felt powerless to stop the rapid decline that was already taking place in his body. Although four more days passed before we said our final farewell, our Lad, the Lad we knew and loved, was already slipping away.

How we wished for just one more walk, one more game of Frisbee, one more day with our beloved boy! He was snatched from us so unexpectedly. We didn't see it coming, but we usually never do. Loss has a way of catching us off guard, and we find ourselves wishing we had placed a little more value on today.

I'm grateful to Lad for teaching me to treasure today and see every moment of this precious life we live as a gift from God. I will never know what tomorrow holds, but I can always choose to treasure and make the most of today.

Lord Jesus, thank You for the gift of today. Please give me eyes to see the opportunities You have prepared for me and arms to embrace the potential that today holds. Amen.

Lad's last neighborhood walk—sixteen months old

LAD LESSON 17: LEARN TO REST

It is vain for you to rise up early, to sit up late, to eat the bread of sorrows; for so He gives His beloved sleep.
—Psalm 127:2

Lad knew when to call it a day. Around 10 p.m., regardless of human activity, he tucked in for the night. My last view each night and my first view every morning was of Lad, belly up in the classic collie sleeping position. We often quipped, "When the boy's out, he's out."

Lad lived every day with gusto. When he was awake, he was ready for action. But once he snuggled into his bed for the night, it took a lot to stir him. He never concerned himself with what hadn't been accomplished or what tomorrow held. Like clockwork, when it was time for bed, that's where Lad was found.

I think that a large portion of Lad's vivacity and vigor in life came from his habit of getting consistent rest. It was as if he knew that strength for each day directly depended on the rest he received each night. Whether Lad thought that deeply about it or not, I will never know. What I do know is that I could definitely benefit from following his example.

I'm thankful to Lad for teaching me that rest should be a priority in my daily routine. It's one of the best ways to prepare for the joys and challenges of tomorrow.

Lord Jesus, thank You for promising to give Your beloved children sleep. Please help me to make adequate rest a consistent part of my daily routine. Amen.

Young Lad using Trustee and Trouper for a pillow

LAD LESSON 18: ANSWER THE CALL

Call upon Me in the day of trouble; I will deliver you, and you shall glorify Me.
—Psalm 50:15

"Laddie!" My voice rang out as Lad vanished over the rolling hills at our favorite romping place, the place we affectionately refer to as The Resort. Within seconds of my call, a ball of sable and white blazed toward me at full speed.

Lad loved to answer my call, and I could count on him to come. Not once did Lad ever fail to fly toward me at the sound of his name. He was always ready and willing to answer my call. Every time. If I needed him, all I had to do was holler, and he would be there in a flash. Lad didn't answer out of mere duty. He answered with sheer delight.

I'm thankful to Lad for teaching me the importance of faithfully answering the call. It's part of building the sacred trust that holds each relationship together.

Lord Jesus, thank You for promising to answer me every time I call on Your name. Thank You for Your great faithfulness and for proving over and over again that You can be trusted. Help me to hear and answer the call of those who need me today. Amen.

Lad celebrating his first birthday at The Resort on March 22, 2021

LAD LESSON 19: WALK WITH POISE

But you, Lord, are a shield around me, my glory, the One who lifts my head high.
—Psalm 3:3 NIV

Lad never just walked. Lad had a spring in his step. His feet appeared to barely touch the ground as he floated from place to place. When we practiced training drills, Lad pranced cheerfully by my side, and it felt like we were dancing together.

Lad walked as though he owned the world. With his head cocked high and his chest puffed out, he often looked like a king surveying his kingdom. Wherever he went, Lad turned heads with his elegant carriage. He possessed an air of grace and confidence that attracted people to him and gave him influence at every turn.

I'm grateful to Lad for teaching me the power of poise. There are a lot of things in life I can't control, but I can always choose how I carry myself and what kind of presence I project to others.

Lord Jesus, thank You for the tangible gift of Your gracious presence in my life. Please help me to walk with a confidence and grace that reflects that I am a child of the King. Amen.

Lad walking the hills of The Resort on his first birthday

LAD LESSON 20: GUARD THE YOUNG

Take heed that you do not despise one of these little ones, for I say to you that in heaven their angels always see the face of My Father who is in heaven.

—Matthew 18:10

Lad's favorite part of every day was running the countryside at The Resort. Acres of rolling hills, saturated with critter smells, thrilled his collie heart. He never tired of exploring this beautiful property and was even more delighted when other family members joined his outdoor adventure.

One day in particular, all three of my nephews, including the youngest one, whom we call Lad's boy, came along for our romp at The Resort. The boys took off over the first hill with a very happy Lad close at their heels. As they ran, he sounded his collie trumpet with shrill bursts of joy. For the duration of our stay, Lad and the boys were in constant motion, darting from one place to another.

The sun was beginning to slip beneath the horizon as we made our way back to the car. We were almost there when I realized that one boy—Lad's boy—was missing, and so was Lad. I rushed back to the top of the first hill to see Lad trailing behind and escorting his boy back to the car. Even when Lad saw me, he never left his boy's side.

I'm thankful to Lad for teaching me by his example to faithfully guard the young. If a young pup like Lad can slow down and walk with a child, so can I.

Lord Jesus, I know that children are precious to You. Please help me to slow down and take time to take care of the little ones in my life. Amen.

Lad with his boy on his half birthday—six months old

LAD LESSON 21: THINK AGAIN

"For My thoughts are not your thoughts, nor are your ways My ways," says the Lord. "For as the heavens are higher than the earth, so are My ways higher than your ways, and My thoughts than your thoughts."
—Isaiah 55:8–9

Lad was a thinker. If something didn't work the first time he tried it, he would stop and think things through again—and again. Watching him attack challenges from multiple angles was first entertaining, then rather inspiring. What would happen if I learned to not just think, but to think again?

Lad manifested this quality most when I introduced new training concepts to him. He never assumed his first attempt was his best one. Failure did not usually frustrate him. If he didn't understand what I wanted, I could see the wheels turning in his soulful eyes, and he would continue to grind on it mentally until he figured it out.

I'm thankful to Lad for teaching me that my first thought is not necessarily my best thought. Thinking my way through a challenge is more powerful than fighting my way through it. Thinking increases my capacity. Learning to think again unleashes creativity and helps me grow toward my potential.

Lord Jesus, please teach me how to think beyond the things that I see and to tap into Your creativity as I navigate the challenges that come my way. Amen.

Lad at The Resort

LAD LESSON 22: CHOOSE TO WAIT

Wait on the Lord; be of good courage, and He shall strengthen your heart; wait, I say, on the Lord!
—Psalm 27:14

One of Lad's earliest lessons was learning to wait. He learned to wait for the invitation to come through an open door, to wait patiently while his food was being served, and to wait for my direction before racing off over the rolling hills on our free walks.

Lad learned rather quickly that waiting patiently was the fastest way to get what he wanted, and as he grew physically, his capacity to wait on me for direction in each situation gradually increased. By the time he was six months old, he had acquired an impressive amount of patience.

The unexpected surprise came when we traveled out west, just before Lad's first birthday. As we explored hundreds of acres of wide-open fields with Lad and Trustee, we noticed something about Lad. Every time we stopped walking, although Trustee would continue to range, Laddie would race back to us, lie down, and wait until we began walking again. We didn't ask him to wait for us. He simply chose to wait.

As Lad grew in his maturity, he moved from learning to wait on us to choosing to wait for us. Each time, our hearts were deeply touched by his choice. I'm thankful to Lad for teaching me that patiently waiting on others is a tangible way to place value on my relationship with them. It's an accomplishment to learn to wait. It's an even greater measure of character to choose to wait.

Lord Jesus, thank You for promising to reward those who wait patiently on You. Please give me the strength to place value on others by choosing to lovingly and patiently wait on them. Amen.

Lad during a romp through the fields in Nebraska—eleven months old

LAD LESSON 23: EMBRACE HARD THINGS

You therefore must endure hardship as a good soldier of Jesus Christ.
—2 Timothy 2:3

Nothing thrilled Lad's collie heart more than a good challenge. Whether it was winning a game of tug-of-war with Trustee or mastering a new obedience drill, Lad thrived on tackling things that were hard. He wasn't looking for an easy win. After all, if it was easy, it wasn't an accomplishment.

Whether he was learning to climb stairs or fishing for a lost toy buried in a pile of brush, Lad was undaunted by difficulty. Even as Lad neared the end of his young life, he still faced hard things with fortitude. As his body and mind began to fail and what had previously been easy became hard, like a faithful soldier, Lad persevered to the very end.

Even on the last leg of his earthly journey, as we entered the vet's office and the small room where we, through many tears, said goodbye to our gallant Lad, he used his remaining strength to press on and to move into the moment before him with courage.

Life is full of challenges. I'm thankful to Lad for teaching me to embrace hard things.

Lord Jesus, give me courage to embrace the opportunities that are present in the difficulties that come my way. Give me strength to take on the challenges of today. Amen.

Lad taking on Trustee and Trouper in a game of tug

LAD LESSON 24: SHAPE GREATNESS

But now, O Lord, You are our Father; we are the clay, and You our potter; and all we are the work of Your hand.

—Isaiah 64:8

Lad was the fulfillment of a dream I had held in my heart for more than twenty-five years. When he joined our pack as an eight-week-old puppy, I was determined to shape Lad for greatness, and I fully believed he would be my finest work. With a long list of training goals in mind, I immediately began teaching him the fundamentals of good character and conduct.

Just six short days after bringing him home, I wrote the following words in my daily journal: "Lad will shape me far more than I will ever shape him." When I penned these words, I had very little understanding of how true they would prove to be. I often wondered at the end of each day if Lad had taught me more than I had attempted to teach him.

Lad's influence on my life was completely positive. Every time I turned around, Lad had a new lesson for me, not only about dog training, but also about life. His resilience, loyalty, sensitivity, kindness, vivacity, determination, and persistence are all qualities I wish to possess in greater measure, and Lad modeled them very well. Lad shaped me far more than I shaped him.

I'm thankful to Lad for teaching me that I have the opportunity every day to shape greatness in others. Time with Lad helped me grow into a better person. I want to have that effect on the people around me.

Lord Jesus, I know it's Your will for my life to have a positive influence on those around me. Please show me how to be part of the beautiful process of shaping another soul for greatness. Amen.

My first portrait with Lad at Carter Collies

LAD LESSON 25: BE GENTLED

Your right hand has held me up, Your gentleness has made me great.

—Psalm 18:35

On July 16, 2020, I wrote: "Lad has gentled me in a way that no other puppy has. I love him deeply." Those words were true then, and they are equally true now. Lad was only three months old at that point, but he had already started to tame my heart in ways that it had never been tamed before.

What made the difference? Was it because he was my first collie, and we tend to view firsts differently? Was it the fact that he had been a dream in my heart long before he was a gift in my hands? I'm not sure what started the massive shift inside of me. I just know that shortly after Lad entered my world, my heart began to change.

I grew less certain of what I thought I knew and more open to what I needed to learn. I listened more—more than I had ever listened before. And the more I listened, the more I learned. The more I learned, the more I realized that I didn't know nearly as much as I thought I knew about training a puppy, or anything else for that matter. The knowledge I had was dwarfed by the knowledge I still lacked.

This was a startling realization. First, it humbled me. Then it began to fill me with a new gentleness of spirit that made it much easier for me to teach Lad and much easier for him to learn.

I'm thankful to Lad for teaching me that gentleness precedes true greatness and that humility is always at the heart of true leadership.

Lord Jesus, Your thoughts and ways are so much greater and higher than mine. Please help me to be humble before You and gentle toward others today. Amen.

Lad at The Resort—nine weeks old

LAD LESSON 26: WALK SOFTLY

Your beauty should not come from outward adornment. . . . Rather, it should be that of your inner self, the unfading beauty of a gentle and quiet spirit, which is of great worth in God's sight.
—1 Peter 3:3–4 NIV

Lad grew rapidly. At just four months old, he was rivaling our golden retriever, Trustee, in height. With his large size, it seemed that it would be impossible for him to enter or exit a room without us hearing the patter of his paws, but not so.

Lad walked softly—so softly that he often came and went without us ever hearing a sound. When he was a young puppy, this sometimes felt frustrating. He sneaked away stealthily without us ever noticing his movement. Lad was so light on his feet that we used to joke that he crept on cat's paws.

As Lad grew older, our appreciation for his soft steps increased. At night, he moved around our room imperceptibly, never once disturbing our sleep. He graced our home daily with the beauty of his quiet ways.

Lad not only walked softly in our home, but he also tread softly in our hearts. He was plenty boisterous when he sensed joy. But when he sensed sadness, Lad came gently to cheer and comfort us with his peaceful presence and soft nuzzles.

Lad showed me that peace and quiet often go together. I'm thankful to Lad for teaching me to walk softly and be a peaceful presence in the lives of those around me.

Lord Jesus, thank You for Your peaceful presence in my life. Help me to keep a quiet heart that brings Your peace to others today. Amen.

Lad taking a stroll at The Resort on his first birthday

LAD LESSON 27: LOVE FIERCELY

My little children, let us not love in word or in tongue, but in deed and in truth.
—1 John 3:18

Loving fiercely was one of Lad's gifts, and he expressed it in ways that were unmistakable. He not only loved me, but he loved everything that smelled like me. Just one week after bringing him home, I glanced over to see nine-week-old Lad sound asleep with his body nestled between my tennis shoes.

By four months of age, Lad's face was full of expression. His eyes were a vast ocean of feeling. Lad loved us with his eyes like no other dog we have ever owned. It was a love full of strength and devotion, a love that he demonstrated daily in dozens of tangible ways—the kind of love that leaves no room for doubt.

Lad was friendly to all, but his love for his family was fierce. We had complete confidence that if we needed him, he'd be there to defend us with zeal.

I'm thankful to Lad for teaching me the importance of expressing my love to others in tangible and unforgettable ways. Lad helped me see the positive difference that even a loving look can make.

Lord Jesus, thank You for loving me fiercely and showing it through Your sacrifice on the cross. Help me to faithfully communicate Your love to those around me today. Amen.

Lad nestled between my tennis shoes—nine weeks old

LAD LESSON 28: BE ALL IN

Whatever your hand finds to do, do it with all your might.
—Ecclesiastes 9:10 NIV

Lad was an all-or-nothing sort of guy. He was either all in or not in at all. If he didn't want to do something, you couldn't force him. If he did want to do something, it was almost impossible to stop him.

In the younger stages of puppyhood, this quality made him quite a handful. But as he grew, it gradually became one of his greatest attributes. When given a job, Lad put every ounce of his energy into it. When he heeled next to me, he did it with flair. When I called him, he came with gusto. When I told him to "leave it," he turned completely away from the temptation.

Lad wasn't wishy-washy. He was very decisive, and once he made a decision, he stood by it. Even when he was not heading in the direction I desired, I still couldn't help but respect his wholehearted devotion. He didn't try to be diplomatic about it either. If he disagreed with me, he showed it openly, and I learned to respect his candid responses. Lad was definitely not a push over.

I'm grateful to Lad for teaching me that wholehearted commitment is better than halfhearted compliance. I valued Lad's cooperation much more because it wasn't automatic. When he chose to submit to my will, it came from a place of strength, not weakness.

Lord Jesus, thank You for being fully devoted to doing Your Father's will. Please give me strength to love and serve You wholeheartedly today. Amen.

Lad tenaciously playing tug with me—nine weeks old

LAD LESSON 29: BE INCLUSIVE

Let all that you do be done with love.

—1 Corinthians 16:14

Call it unquenchable curiosity or extreme sociability, but Lad didn't leave anyone out. He made everyone feel included.

Up until Lad, all my dogs had been exclusively devoted to me. Even if they weren't one-person dogs, they still showed a distinct preference for my company. After all, I fed them, exercised them, and cared for them. They knew who bought their kibble.

Lad did not follow that pattern at all. If family members were scattered all over the house, he made his rounds from one to the other, consistently checking in with everyone. I didn't always know who Lad was hanging out with, but I did know that he was always with somebody. And he had an uncanny sense of who needed his company the most.

When I took him places, Lad responded warmly to everyone. He loved without partiality. Sometimes this trait sparked a little jealousy in my heart. I wanted to be his special person. But looking back, I see how much I can learn from Lad's example.

I'm thankful to Lad for teaching me that real love is inclusive. His love for others never took away from his love for me. Each person in our family had their own special place in his heart. His life had a greater impact because his love was inclusive.

Lord Jesus, thank You for Your limitless love for me and for the opportunities You give me every day to share Your love with others. Amen.

Lad surrounded by some of his favorite people

LAD LESSON 30: TRUST THROUGH PAIN

Trust in the Lord with all your heart, and lean not on your own understanding; in all your ways acknowledge Him, and He shall direct your paths.

—Proverbs 3:5–6

From day one, free walks at The Resort were a consistent part of Lad's daily routine. Watching him sprint across the rolling hills with Trustee was a beautiful sight to behold. As the saying goes, a tired puppy is a good puppy. And Lad was always good and tired when we returned home.

After one of our delightful romps, we found a tick latched onto Lad in a rather tender place. He was only two months old at the time, and I knew that it would be a challenge to remove it, head and all. Each time I almost had the burrowed tick out, Lad squirmed, and I had to start the process all over again.

While I worked delicately, trying not to cause him more pain than was necessary, it occurred to me that it takes more strength to trust through pain than it does to trust through pleasure. Finally, my patience paid off, and Lad lay there calmly while I successfully removed the tick from his small body. This was the first time, but not the last, that Lad allowed me to do something that hurt to protect him from something that had the potential to cause him greater harm. Each time, I was deeply touched that he was willing to trust me.

I'm thankful to Lad for teaching me that pain is a greater test of trust than pleasure and that things that hurt momentarily may be necessary to protect me from something that could cause lasting harm.

Lord Jesus, please give me strength to trust You through the pain that Your love allows. Help me to remember that pain is sometimes a necessary part of accomplishing Your loving purpose in my life. Amen.

Lad on his two-month birthday

LAD LESSON 31: BE TALL INSIDE

But speaking the truth in love, we are to grow up in all aspects into Him who is the head, that is, Christ.
—Ephesians 4:15 NASB

From the moment we first set eyes on Lad on May 15, 2020, his inward stature stood out to us. His sizable personality spilled out of his rather small puppy frame and captured us instantly.

As Lad grew, his inner growth continued to outpace his outer growth, which was impressive considering his rapid growth physically. Lad's intuition was remarkable. We rarely had to explain things to him. Like Albert Payson Terhune's famous collie, whose name he bore, Lad just seemed to understand.

At only three months old, Lad aced the very first training video we ever shot together—on his first try! He took something that was completely unrehearsed and made it look scripted. Lad also had an eerie ability to discern when he was on the job. The moment his "work hat" was on, he instantly transformed from playful puppy to dependable working partner.

Lad's greatness of heart was best seen in his treatment of small children. Although not easily mastered by adults, Lad was very meek in the presence of little people. Nothing filled Lad's collie heart with more contentment than tiny fingers fondling his luxurious coat.

Lad was tall on the outside, but he was even taller on the inside. I'm thankful to Lad for teaching me that inner character counts more than physical stature.

Lord Jesus, please help me to place more value on inner character than on outward appearance. Teach me how to grow taller on the inside today. Amen.

Lad's last time sitting on my lap for a Sunday portrait—six months old

LAD LESSON 32: BE HELPFUL

God is our refuge and strength, an ever-present help in trouble.
—Psalm 46:1 NIV

Lad loved being helpful. Sometimes his attempts were more comical than useful, but he constantly looked for ways to lend us a paw.

If we picked up sticks, Lad started scouting for his own. If a fly invaded the house, he did his best to catch it for us. If we failed to notice something important, Lad "told" us about it. When lifting Lad into the car, he helped by placing his two front paws on the tailgate. I'm convinced that if Lad could've figured out how to help us cook dinner, he would've done that too.

When life got too serious, Lad grabbed a toy to help lighten things up. When it was mealtime, Lad took his place between David and me and lay down calmly at our feet. Sometimes Lad would even crate himself when he sensed that we were getting ready to leave.

Once Lad knew what was expected of him in a given situation, we didn't need to direct him. Sometimes he was even one step ahead of my thought process, anticipating what I needed him to do next. Lad did his part to carry his own weight and make life easier for us.

I'm thankful to Lad for teaching me to be more aware of how I can offer assistance to those around me. He proved that being helpful in little ways can make a big difference.

Lord Jesus, thank You for promising to be a very present help in times of trouble. Please help me to notice the needs of others today, and give me a heart that is ready and willing to be helpful. Amen.

Lad fetching a stick and his favorite ball at the same time

LAD LESSON 33: PRESS PAUSE

The Lord is good to those who wait for Him, to the soul who seeks Him.
—Lamentations 3:25

When Lad joined our pack as an eight-week-old puppy, he brought a flurry of happy activity to our home. Weeks rapidly rolled into months, and it felt like every time I blinked, he was bigger. I was living my dream of owning a collie, and I loved musing on the things Lad and I would do and the places we would go together.

Then unexpectedly, everything changed. With no warning, Lad had a series of grand mal seizures and didn't recover. My world stopped. Everything that had been so important just moments before suddenly didn't even register weight on the scale.

For the next five days, I spent hours holding Lad on my lap, stroking his forehead, fondling his silky ears, and running my fingers through his thick sable-and-white coat. Time suddenly didn't feel like it even existed as I watched my rambunctious and lively Lad degenerate into a clumsy, disoriented, lethargic shadow of what he had been just days before.

During the last week of Lad's life, I pressed pause. I paused in a way I should have many times before, but didn't. And I don't regret one minute of it. What I do regret is waiting to press pause until it was necessary.

I'm thankful to Lad for teaching me the importance of pressing pause regularly and taking inventory of the things that truly matter to me. If I press pause when I don't need to, I will be without regrets when life requires it.

Lord Jesus, thank You for Your promise to be good to those who wait on You. Help my use of time to reflect my true values today. Amen.

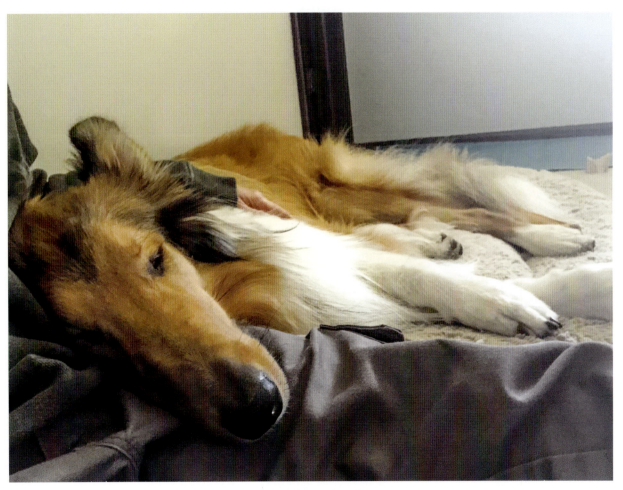
Final days with Lad

LAD LESSON 34: NOTICE THE LITTLE THINGS

Are not two little sparrows sold for a penny? And yet not one of them will fall to the ground without your Father's leave (consent) and notice. But even the very hairs of your head are all numbered. Fear not, then; you are of more value than many sparrows.

—Matthew 10:29–31 AMPC

Lad noticed the little things. I remember the day he discovered insects for the first time. Bounding after butterflies on our free walks instantly became one of his favorite forms of self-entertainment.

Wherever I took Lad, he constantly helped me rediscover the small wonders of the beautiful world that God created. From the tiniest ant crawling on the ground to the little leaf carried by the wind, Lad noticed it all.

One night Lad "told" me about a spider he spotted on the ceiling of my bedroom. As I was sitting on my bed unwinding from a busy day, Lad strolled over to my side and looked at me, then up toward the ceiling. He repeated this action until I traced his gaze to a tiny spider. Then, as if his job was done, he peacefully settled back down on his bed.

Lad's awareness reached beyond the physical realm. He recognized our moments of joy and never missed out on a good joke. He also sensed our sorrow and swiftly offered comfort. Lad's perception was sharp and his curiosity insatiable—two traits that will always stand out in my memory. Sometimes Lad was more keenly aware of what was happening inside of me than I was.

I'm thankful to Lad for teaching me the value of noticing the little things. It's often the little things that have the capacity to make a big difference in daily life.

Lord Jesus, thank You for caring about the smallest details of my life. Help me to notice the little things that have the potential to make a big difference in the lives of others. Amen.

Lad's gotcha day at Carter Collies—eight weeks old

LAD LESSON 35: ASK WHY

Evildoers do not understand what is right, but those who seek the Lord understand it fully.
—Proverbs 28:5 NIV

Lad was my first real taste of owning a herding dog. By nature he came with a unique set of instincts and behaviors that went along with the territory. The major challenge was trying to understand behaviors that my previous puppies had never displayed. My Labrador and golden retrievers had not prepared me for a puppy that had an innate desire to round up the family using rapid agility and teeth.

I vividly remember the morning that his needlelike puppy teeth nailed the back of my heel as I strolled across the kitchen to warm my coffee. Ouch! Reacting came very naturally to me, but only seemed to add to Lad's fun of nipping at my heels.

After some failed attempts to curb this and other undesirable traits, I started to ask myself why. Why is Lad doing what he is doing? This question helped me trace his behaviors back to the herding tendencies that are an inherent part of his breed's composition. This question also became useful for other situations in which Lad was acting in ways that were out of the box. Each time I paused long enough to ask why, I gained insight that enabled me to respond to Lad in ways that were more helpful to him.

I'm thankful to Lad for teaching me that understanding the whys helps me choose a wise response to situations that I don't automatically understand.

Lord Jesus, thank You for promising to give understanding to those who seek You. Help me to be wise by trying to understand the whys behind what others do today. Amen.

Lad unleashing some of his fury on Trustee

LAD LESSON 36: CALMER IS BETTER

He who has knowledge spares his words, and a man of understanding is of a calm spirit.
—Proverbs 17:27

I was not born calm, so this lesson did not come easily for me. Yet Lad helped me learn this quality better than any other dog I have ever trained.

There was only one sure fire way of maintaining control of Lad, and that was to remain calm even when Lad was acting crazy. In fact, losing control of my emotions was the quickest way to lose control of Lad. Although I have gradually grown stronger in this area of life, Lad lifted me to a whole new level.

Lad's explosive energy and extreme intelligence required me to maintain a sharp leadership edge. If Lad sensed even small undercurrents of frustration or impatience in me, he became much less cooperative.

Most of what he did was all in fun—at least from his perspective. From my perspective, however, many of his behaviors were not funny. At all. Sometimes my rash responses were highly entertaining to Lad and provided more of an incentive than a deterrent for his actions.

I'm grateful to Lad for teaching me that staying calmer is always better. Maintaining a right attitude is more powerful than manufacturing right actions. Choosing to stay calm and in control of myself will always give me the greatest amount of influence in any situation.

Lord Jesus, thank You for teaching me the value of self-control. Please help me to remain calm under pressure today. Amen.

Lad on his three-month birthday

LAD LESSON 37: LIFE IS THE GIFT

For the wages of sin is death; but the gift of God is eternal life through Jesus Christ our Lord.
—Romans 6:23 KJV

Lad was full of life! He added to our days in ways that escaped our awareness until we lost him. Nothing was redundant to Lad. He never lost the wonder of waking up and jumping into each day as though it were his very first. The routine walks at The Resort never grew old. To Lad, each romp over the rolling hills was a brand-new adventure.

When packages arrived by the dozens leading up to our wedding, Lad wanted a front-row seat as we opened each one. Although none of them were for him, he nosed his way under my arm and watched with anticipation as the contents were unpacked. Lad found the extraordinary in the ordinary, and living never lost its charm.

During the last five days of Lad's life, I sat on the floor with him for hours watching the rise and fall of his chest with every breath. I felt the warmth of his body against mine and thanked God for each precious moment. Lad could no longer do all the things he loved to do, but it did not diminish his love for life. He still embraced life to the fullest to the very end. To Lad, life was the gift—no other amenities were needed.

In Lad's final moments, I held him in my arms. His breathing slowed and then stopped, and something more tangible but less visible than his body left: life. Everything I had grown so visibly attached to was still there. But the most precious of all things was gone, and I was powerless to bring it back.

I'm thankful to Lad for teaching me that life is not just a gift, but it is *the* gift—the gift without which no other gifts can be received or enjoyed. Nothing is more precious than life.

Lord Jesus, thank You for giving me the gift of life—not only earthly life, but also the gift of eternal life with You. Please help me see each moment of life as a gift to be received with gratitude. Amen.

Lad eagerly anticipating the opening of the next wedding package

LAD LESSON 38: TRUST YOUR GUT

Your ears shall hear a word behind you, saying, "This is the way, walk in it," whenever you turn to the right hand or whenever you turn to the left.

—Isaiah 30:21

Lad's first birthday was just around the corner, and this imminent event sparked happy chatter about how we could best celebrate with our gallant boy. After some deliberation, we settled on a plan that we knew would delight Lad more than all the other birthday frills or festivities we could muster.

So we reserved the date, prayed for nice weather, and prepared to capture some pictures of Lad enjoying a rendezvous at his favorite country place. When the day arrived, the weather was indeed perfect, and everything seemed to be running on schedule. That is, until a last-minute family invitation rolled in.

We immediately felt torn in two different directions. Family is a top priority in our lives, and it went against the grain of our logic to put Lad's birthday outing above spending the evening with family. But something in our gut urged us even more strongly to stick with our original plan. So we loaded up the pack and headed off to The Resort.

Lad had a grand time exploring all the sights, smells, and sounds of a world awakening from a long winter's nap, and we loved every minute of watching him revel in all things dog. Of course, at the time, we never imagined that Lad's first birthday would be his last birthday with us or that the pictures we took of him that evening would be among the fondest memories we have of his life.

I'm grateful to Lad for teaching me that even though I don't know the future, I can trust God, who knows the end from the beginning, to give me the internal guidance I need.

Lord Jesus, please help me to trust the guidance You give, even when it doesn't make sense at the moment. Give me a gut-feel for Your will. Amen.

Lad reveling in a romp at The Resort on his first birthday

LAD LESSON 39: SEEK PEACE

Therefore let us pursue the things which make for peace and the things by which one may edify another.
—Romans 14:19

Although Lad was not always peaceful, he was always a seeker of peace. Lad disliked conflict and did his best, albeit not always successfully, to avoid it.

I have two vivid memories that center around Lad's pursuit of peace. The first is my morning prayer time. It was not uncommon for Lad to rest his front paws and head on the back of my legs as I knelt beside my bed to talk with God. He is the first and only dog I have ever had that loved to draw near to me during prayer.

The second memory is of Lad lying contentedly under our baby grand piano while I played hymns and personal compositions. This is often my way of decompressing after a stressful day, and Lad embraced the acoustical vibrations of the piano and the peace that came along with each musical moment.

I'm grateful to Lad for teaching me that peace is something I can pursue daily. When I seek peace, I will press into the moments where peace is present.

Lord Jesus, thank You for giving me peace that passes all understanding. Make my life a place that brings Your peace to others today. Amen.

Lad with Trouper and Trustee at The Resort–six months old

LAD LESSON 40: FOCUS ON THE GIFT

The Lord gave, and the Lord has taken away; blessed be the name of the Lord.

—Job 1:21

Joy. That's what Lad brought. The kind that filled my heart and spilled out over the edges of my soul. The first time I took him in my arms, the bond was forged, and it felt like, from eternity past, Lad was created just for me.

Loss. It was an unwelcome intruder in my life. It came without permission. It took away from me something that nothing could replace and that I had no power to recover. It ravaged my dream and robbed me of my beloved Lad before he was fully grown.

Grief. That's what losing Lad brought. Grief in proportions I had never before known. Pain that ran deeper than my heart could feel, leaving me with a sense of emptiness and emotional numbness that words can't even describe. Like ocean waves, some violent and some more gentle, grief kept rolling over my bereaved heart—grief as unpredictable as the loss that caused it.

A gift. That's what Lad was. As Lad's second birthday approached, my heart wrestled with the still unthinkable reality of his death. In the midst of the gut-wrenching sorrow I felt, the question came to me: Will I focus on the grief, or will I focus on the gift? Had I known how soon I would have to part with Lad, would I have chosen to forgo the joy of loving him to escape the grief of losing him?

The grief of losing Lad is only this great because the gift of having him was even greater. What God gave me in Lad is something that can never be taken away. I'm grateful for how this loss is teaching me, in the midst of grief, to focus on and be grateful for the gift.

Lord Jesus, whether You give or whether You take away, give me strength to choose gratitude and to bless Your name. Please give me grace to focus on Your gifts today. Amen.

Lad at The Resort after a free walk—nine weeks old

LAD LESSON 41: TRY NEW THINGS

But the people that do know their God shall be strong, and do exploits.
—Daniel 11:32 KJV

Lad was not afraid to try new things. Exploring new places, meeting new people, playing with new toys, and learning new games were all on his favorites list.

Just before Lad's first birthday, we traveled out west to spend a full week with our cousins in Nebraska. It was Lad's first time down on the farm, and he embraced it instantly. With more than seven hundred acres of wide-open fields to explore, Lad was in doggy paradise!

Many fabulous firsts peppered Lad's days on the farm, including his first time drinking out of a water hydrant and his first time being in close proximity to cats, chickens, and other farm critters.

The most memorable event, though, was his first encounter with a herd of cattle. They had met a dog before, but it was quite obvious that Lad had never met a cow. Slowly and cautiously, he took a few tentative steps forward as his nose twitched rapidly, trying to take in the new scent. Gradually, Lad gained more confidence until he was standing nose to nose with a steer.

Lad's short life was fuller and better because he stepped outside of his comfort zone. I'm thankful to Lad for teaching me that life is not a spectator sport. It's an adventure to be lived. Lad kept his life and ours far more interesting because he was willing to try new things.

Lord Jesus, please rescue me from the rut of living life within my comfort zone. Give me courage to try something new or reach out to someone new today. Amen.

Lad's first time nose to nose with a steer—eleven months old

LAD LESSON 42: FORGIVE QUICKLY

And be kind to one another, tenderhearted, forgiving one another, even as God in Christ forgave you.
—Ephesians 4:32

No one who knew Lad could deny that he had a fiery temper. Like an unpredictable storm at sea, we never knew what would trigger his next outburst.

No matter how gentle my approach to grooming was, Lad still saw the brush as an instrument of torture. The slightest tug of his hair sent him into a tizzy. And heaven help anyone who accidentally stepped on Lad's paw! The day our poor golden retriever, Trustee, made that unfortunate mistake, a blur of snarling teeth followed. A split second later, all was well and Lad was sweet again.

Lad's tendency toward tantrums was beautifully offset by his readiness to forgive. He never held a grudge. No matter how big the perceived offense was, he was always quick to forgive and continue loving.

Lad sought forgiveness quickly anytime he sensed that I was unhappy with him. Resting his chin on me, he would gaze up with soulful eyes until I assured him, "It's okay, Laddie. I forgive you."

I'm grateful to Lad for teaching me that one of the most powerful ways to preserve relationships is to readily forgive and seek forgiveness from others. Lad lived a better life because he did not hang on to past hurts.

Lord Jesus, thank You for Your sacrificial death on the cross and making a way for me to be forgiven. As You have forgiven me, please give me grace to freely and fully forgive those who cause me pain. Amen.

Lad "nosing up" to Trustee—nine weeks old

LAD LESSON 43: BE FULLY PRESENT

"Behold, the virgin shall be with child, and bear a Son, and they shall call His name Immanuel," which is translated, "God with us."

—Matthew 1:23

Present. That's one of the top words I would use to describe Lad. He filled my life with his presence every day in ways that were both memorable and meaningful.

One evening, my heart was breaking over something extremely painful. After collapsing on the floor in a puddle of emotion, almost instantly I felt Lad standing next to me with his warm fur brushing gently against my cheek. Without hesitation, Lad fully stepped into my moment of pain and pressed into me as I wrapped my arms around him and buried my face in the thick scruff of his neck. There he stood, firmly and quietly, until I found the strength to rise again.

Lad gave me the only gift that had value at that moment—himself. The power was not in what he did, but it was in what he chose to be. In times of extreme joy or deep sorrow and all the moments in between, Lad sensed what was happening in the hearts around him and offered the gift of his presence.

I'm thankful to Lad for modeling what it means to be fully present in the lives of those I love. It's easy to get caught up in the doing and lose sight of the power of being the person whom others need.

Lord Jesus, thank You for Your faithful and loving presence in my life. I'm grateful for all You do for me, but I treasure most who You are. Help me to be fully present in the lives of those who need me today. Amen.

Lad—five months old

LAD LESSON 44: LOVE LIGHT

Then Jesus spoke to them again, saying, "I am the light of the world. He who follows Me shall not walk in darkness, but have the light of life."

—John 8:12

Lad loved light. Unless it was time for bed, he did not like darkness at all.

When the sun went to sleep, so did Lad, and he greeted each morning with joy. After dark, Lad often refused to move forward until I placed light on his path. He stood like a statue until he could see what lay ahead of him.

Lad's love of light became even more apparent as our first Christmas season with him approached. From the moment the lights were strung on the Christmas tree, it was his favorite place to be. Even as a nine-month-old puppy, still quite full of mischief, he never touched a single ornament or messed with the garland-laden branches. He simply curled up under the Christmas tree with the low-hanging branches almost tickling his ears.

As the gifts began to fill the Christmas tree skirt, Lad still found ways to wedge himself under the tree and bask in the gentle glow of the lights. It was hard to tell who was more disappointed when the Christmas decorations came down that year—me or Lad.

Lad was drawn to more than physical light. He gravitated toward people who radiated the light of love, joy, and peace in their lives.

I'm thankful to Lad for teaching me to be a lover of light. I want my life to be full of the kind of light that helps others see and brings life to those around me.

Lord Jesus, You are the Light of the World. Please help me to live in such a way that others see Your light and experience Your life through me. Amen.

Lad enjoying his first Christmas—nine months old

LAD LESSON 45: BE MERRY

A merry heart does good, like medicine, but a broken spirit dries the bones.

—Proverbs 17:22

Lad's enthusiasm for life was contagious. He bounded into every day with a joy that could barely be contained.

As a young pup, Lad displayed curiosity that kept me on my toes constantly. As an adolescent, he delighted in being silly with his toys, often glancing up to see if he had an audience. Making me burst into gales of laughter seemed to be one of his main objectives, and it filled him with ecstasy every time he succeeded. He tenaciously tickled me with his antics and refused to give up until it was impossible for me to suppress the giggles bubbling up inside.

His merry heart kept the atmosphere of our home light, even when the responsibilities of the day felt heavy. I remember looking at him and thinking, *You are such good medicine!* And he truly was.

I'm thankful to Lad for teaching me the huge difference a merry heart can make. I had never thought of laughter as a gift to give to others until I received that gift daily from Lad.

Lord Jesus, please show me how to bring Your joy to those around me. Help me to choose to have a merry heart today. Amen.

Lad with one of his favorite toys

LAD LESSON 46: SHARE YOUR TOYS

He who did not spare His own Son, but delivered Him up for us all, how shall He not with Him also freely give us all things?

—Romans 8:32

Most dogs like to hoard what they have, but Lad was a rare exception. He genuinely loved to share, and this generous trait was visible from a very young age.

Lad viewed everything as a team sport. From Lad's perspective, a good game of retrieving involved giving everyone who was present an opportunity to toss the toy. Captured on video is four-month-old Lad taking his toy to a different person after each retrieve, and he did a fairly good job of doling out equal opportunity.

Even during pack play with our two golden retrievers, Lad loved to share his stick, his tug toy, or anything else that he considered part of the game. Being generous just came naturally to him, and he lived by the motto "The more the merrier."

I'm grateful to Lad for teaching me that possessions bring more joy when they are freely shared with others. Giving is the key to more abundant living.

Lord Jesus, thank You for sharing Your wealth with me. As I have freely received blessings from Your gracious hand, may I be faithful to freely share this abundance with others. Amen.

Lad sharing his Frisbee with Trustee and Trouper—six months old

LAD LESSON 47: BE CREATIVE

"You are worthy, O Lord, to receive glory and honor and power; for You created all things, and by Your will they exist and were created."

—Revelation 4:11

Creative? That's not a word I would've ever thought to apply to a dog until Lad entered my life. I've owned several dogs and trained dozens, but Lad is the first one that distinctly exhibited the quality of creativity.

Lad creatively entertained himself. One day, after many futile attempts to get Trustee and Trouper engaged in some form of recreation, Lad latched onto the rope hanging from the swing set, and a lively game of tug-of-war followed. Peering out the window, I watched with amusement as his creativity conquered boredom. The swing set won, of course, but that didn't stop Lad from having a good time.

Lad exercised creativity when he encountered obstacles. He welcomed a good problem and did not allow failure to succeed in dampening his spirit. His curiosity and creativity would take over, and troubleshooting the problem became his entertainment.

Lad was creative in building relationships. He found ways to connect with all people and altered his approach based on each person's disposition. Rejection didn't faze him. It was never a matter of whether someone would like him; it was only a matter of when. He adjusted his demeanor to winsomely wiggle his way into just about anyone's heart.

I'm grateful to Lad for teaching me that being creative is a better use of energy than being reactive. When something stood in Lad's way, he put his energy into creativity.

Lord Jesus, thank You for all that You have created and for the creativity You have built into the things You have made. Please help me to reflect Your character by thinking creatively today. Amen.

Lad at The Resort—three months old

LAD LESSON 48: GRIEF IS GRIEF

Yea, though I walk through the valley of the shadow of death, I will fear no evil; for You are with me; Your rod and Your staff, they comfort me.

—Psalm 23:4

Loss is an inevitable part of life, but some losses affect us more than others. The loss of Lad sliced so deeply through my heart that I could not measure the extent of the wound. None of my previous losses had prepared me for this one.

Following Lad's death, there were days when I could barely function. I often felt present physically, but absent mentally and emotionally. Life went on around me, but nothing was moving forward within me. I experienced a strange mixture of inexpressible grief, mind-numbing heartache, and anger—yes, anger—accompanied by feelings I didn't want to feel and thoughts I didn't want to think. I felt an intense desire to change what I couldn't change and a lack of strength to change the things that I could. There were times when I thought I was finally breaking through to some light, followed by days when all that light was eclipsed by the darkness of my loss.

The most surprising emotion, though, was the guilt that compounded as I compared my loss to that of friends and family members who had endured the loss of so much more. In a moment of raw honesty, I confessed this sense of guilt to my husband, who had lost his only brother to leukemia. I felt so foolish grieving the loss of my dog when that loss could in no way compare with David losing his sibling. That's when David took me in his arms and quietly spoke three words: "Grief is grief."

Those words have left their mark on my heart. Comparison is futile when it comes to grief. Grief is a process, and the feelings that come with it are real regardless of who or what or why you are grieving. I'm thankful that through the loss of Lad, I'm learning that grief is grief and that comparing one loss to another will never help the heart to heal.

Lord Jesus, thank You for promising to be with me when I walk through the valley of the shadow of death. Please make me a place of compassion for those who are grieving a loss in their life today. Amen.

Final moments with Lad on August 5, 2021

LAD LESSON 49: FIND YOUR OFF SWITCH

He who is slow to anger is better than the mighty, and he who rules his spirit than he who takes a city.
—Proverbs 16:32

Lad's excitement level could skyrocket quickly. Rapid motion of any kind triggered his impulse to chase. His intense personality, combined with his agility, made him tough competition, even for his canine companions. Lad was always determined to win.

When Lad and I walked the beautiful hills at The Resort, I loved to wait until he was a good distance away and then take off running in the opposite direction as fast as my legs could carry me. It was like watching a blur of fur racing in my direction as his ground-covering stride devoured the turf between us. His hot pursuit was never a quiet one either. It was always punctuated with shrill barks. But the moment I stopped moving, he would screech to a halt and land a polite sit, his eyes still dancing with playfulness.

Lad's indomitable disposition would've made him completely unmanageable if it were not for one redeeming factor: Lad had a good "off switch," and he knew how to find it quickly. Even as a young puppy, he had the strength to bring himself back under control in a matter of seconds. I could depend on his ability to find his off switch, and that made him a safe playmate and a stellar working partner.

I'm grateful to Lad for teaching me that passion and intensity are winning qualities as long as they are tempered by a good off switch. Too much passion is rarely the problem; the problem is too little self-control.

Lord Jesus, thank You for the passion You displayed as You lived Your life on this earth and died on the cross to purchase my salvation. Give me strength to rule my own spirit well today. Amen.

Lad running to me on a recall—seven months old

LAD LESSON 50: BE OPTIMISTIC

Now may the God of hope fill you with all joy and peace in believing, that you may abound in hope by the power of the Holy Spirit.

—Romans 15:13

Lad was an eternal optimist. From his perspective, every day held endless opportunities. And if the opportunities did not come to him, he chased them down. No matter how many times I declined his invitation to play, he still clung to the hope that the game he desired was just on the other side of the "brick wall."

Hope and expectation colored his lens of the world. Lad hoped constantly, and it was written all over his face. Such hope was hard to disappoint and often influenced the course of my day. Disappointments had little impact on his outlook. In fact, they only served as a springboard for greater anticipation. If I could've placed a caption on the eager expression he wore, it would read, "What are we going to do next?"

Lad's happy-go-lucky disposition was largely shaped by his relentless belief that the next good thing was waiting just around the corner. I'm thankful to Lad for teaching me to focus on the prospects ahead of me instead of the problems in front of me. It's a much better way to live.

Lord Jesus, thank You for being the God of hope. Help my perspective on life to consistently reflect the eternal hope that I have in You. Amen.

Lad looking up at me expectantly during a family gathering—five months old

LAD LESSON 51: EASY ISN'T ALWAYS BEST

Looking unto Jesus, the author and finisher of our faith, who for the joy that was set before Him endured the cross, despising the shame, and has sat down at the right hand of the throne of God.

—Hebrews 12:2

What is best is not always easy, and what is easy is not always best. It was excruciatingly painful to hold Lad in my arms as he took his final breath, but it was best, and I wouldn't trade those moments with him for anything in the world.

It was even more difficult to dig Lad's grave, place him in it, and begin piling the dirt on top of his lifeless body. Each shovelful felt ten times heavier than it actually was as my body heaved with sobs. Yet the grieving that happened in those moments and the closure they brought were a valuable part of helping my heart begin to let go.

Watching our golden retriever, Trustee, pay respects to his protégé was heart-wrenching. However, Trustee needed to be there and to know exactly what had happened to the puppy into which he had poured so much of his life over the past fourteen months.

None of this was easy, but all of it was best. I'm thankful to Lad for teaching me that running from what is hard never makes it easier. Refusing to feel never helps the heart to heal. Pressing into pain, not pulling back from it, begins the arduous process of putting the broken pieces of the heart back together.

Lord Jesus, thank You for being willing to be touched by my pain. When You died for me on the cross, You did not choose what was easy; You chose what was best. Give me courage to press into the pain Your love allows and strength to embrace those around me who are hurting today. Amen.

We all stood in silence as Trustee paid respects to Lad

Trustee's final farewell to Lad

LAD LESSON 52: ASSUME YOU DON'T KNOW

The way of fools seems right to them, but the wise listen to advice.

—Proverbs 12:15 NIV

This may be the most valuable lesson Lad taught me: Assume you don't know.

For the vast majority of Lad's fourteen months with me, I made the assumption that I knew everything I needed to know to train him well. After all, I'm a dog trainer. I know how to train puppies, right? But looking in the rearview mirror, I now see how much I didn't know and how much I still have to learn.

I didn't know that Lad's behavioral issues were symptoms of a neurological condition. But as I sat with him in the emergency vet clinic in the early morning hours of August 2, 2021, all the pieces of the puzzle started to fit together.

His precocious personality. His unpredictable fits of temper. His incredibly sweet and shockingly sassy moments. His strong aversion to being brushed. His random reactions to touch. All these things were indications of something I didn't know, something he couldn't control. I was blind to what I didn't know because I thought I already knew.

My cousin shared a thought with me that captures it well: "When we know better, we do better." But if we already think we know, we never try to know better, which means we never move toward doing better.

What would happen if I replaced criticism with honest curiosity or rash judgments with genuine interest? What would happen if I substituted sincere questions for automatic assumptions? What would happen if in every situation I developed the default of assuming I don't know?

How grateful I am to Lad for teaching me to assume I don't know! The realization that my knowledge is imperfect raises my awareness that there is always something more to learn.

Lord Jesus, help me to ask more questions rather than relying on what I think I know. Teach me to look to You for wisdom in every situation I face and to always assume that I don't know all that there is to know. Amen.

Lad on his seven-month birthday

EPILOGUE: CHOOSE TO LOVE AGAIN

There is no fear in love; but perfect love casts out fear.
— 1 John 4:18

To love again—is this not one of the greatest fears of a heart that has been shattered by loss?

Almost a year passed between our parting with Lad and our selection of a new puppy. I felt joy and anticipation, especially when I realized that a year to the day we lost our Lad, we would be holding Lad's Legend, our next collie puppy, in our arms. It felt like redeeming grace for God to take a day marked by grief and fill our hearts and hands with a new little life to love.

As the puppy pick-up day approached and we started packing for our journey to North Carolina, my heart began to fall apart. I suddenly felt afraid—afraid to love again. The frightening realization that to open my heart to love is to open my heart to loss almost paralyzed me emotionally.

I seriously wondered, *Can I love another puppy?* Everything within me wanted to pull back from the thought of further pain. But what would happen if, in an effort to avoid loss, I close my heart to love? What kind of life would that be? As I struggled through the deep waters of grief all over again, I began to pray. I prayed that God would give me courage to love again.

I'm grateful that through the gift of Lad's Legend, I'm learning how life-giving it is to love again. Fear and love are incompatible with each other. To choose to love again is the best antidote to the fear of loss.

Dear Lord Jesus, thank You for loving me perfectly and for not fearing the loss that Your love for me required. Please give me the strength to love again, no matter how much loss touches my life. Help me to love others just as You have loved me. Amen.

This is love: not that we loved God, but that he loved us and sent his Son as an atoning sacrifice for our sins.
— 1 John 4:10 NIV

For God so loved the world that He gave His only begotten Son, that whoever believes in Him should not perish but have everlasting life.
— John 3:16

One of my first pictures with Lad's Legend on August 5, 2022, a year to the day we lost our Lad

Sunday portrait with Lad's Legend—four months old

Photo by Michael Wesco

ABOUT THE AUTHOR

Christine Nicole Ferris calls Indiana home. Ten years of participation in the Elkhart County 4-H program cultivated a love for public speaking and canine training, two passions that have shaped her life and career as a canine leadership trainer.

    From an early age, Christine's dogs became one of God's richest classrooms for developing her character, and they continue to play a significant role in her personal growth on a daily basis. Her walk with Christ has been deepened as aspects of her relationship with God have become more tangible through her work with the many dogs she has owned and trained.

    Christine and her husband, David, love to start each day with Bible time, prayer, and a good cup of coffee. Together they team up to teach leadership principles with a canine component and thrive on serving their community in as many ways as possible with their two golden retrievers, Trustee and Trouper, and their rough collie, Lad's Legend.

www.LessonsFromLad.com

www.Facebook.com/LessonsFromLad

Contact: LessonsFromLad@gmail.com

Order Information

To order additional copies of this book, please visit
www.redemption-press.com.
Also available at Amazon, Christian bookstores,
and Barnes and Noble.